Wonderful Geoffrey —

Thanks for being our
official Wedding Skipper!
And for being a
wonderful brother.

Lots of love,
Kath & Steve

Lakeland
VIEWS

VAL CORBETT

MYRIAD BOOKS LONDON

CONTENTS

WINDERMERE, ESTHWAITE AND CONISTON

Windermere is the largest and busiest lake in the Lake District. By contrast Esthwaite, its small neighbour, is a quiet haunt for fishermen. Coniston is notable for its literary connections

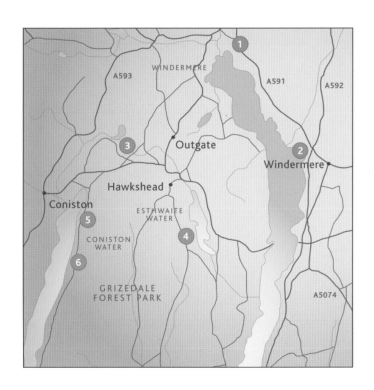

OPPOSITE – CONISTON REEDS
The reflections of reeds and branches are attractively interlaced on the lake's edge near Peel Island

WINDERMERE BOATS

A calm winter dawn at Waterhead, Ambleside gives little indication of the same scene later in the day when the lake will be busy with the comings and goings of small craft and launches. The whole 11 mile (18 km) length of the lake becomes even busier in the summer when the larger boats, *Swan*, *Teal* and *Tern* are in service.

WINDERMERE

Queen Adelaide's Hill on the east shore of the lake is one of the most accessible places away from the main road and gives this view of Windermere and its surrounding fells. The traditional white house at Millerground (centre) is close to one of the public landing stages. Since the introduction of the 10 mph speed limit on the lake, Windermere now better reflects the National Park's policy of 'quiet enjoyment'.

TARN HOWS

Despite the enormous popularity of this beauty spot, the path around Tarn Hows gives lovely intimate views of the many peaceful little bays. The path is suitable for buggies and wheelchairs – although for un-motorised wheelchairs the steeper sections may require an extra assistant. Short climbs onto the surrounding slopes reveal excellent views to the Coniston Fells, the Langdale Pikes (centre) and the Fairfield Horseshoe.

ESTHWAITE WATER

Esthwaite is in the heart of Beatrix Potter country and her home at Hill Top in Near Sawrey is just a short step from the small lake. Hereabouts the little hummocky knolls, topped with trees, are instantly familiar from her illustrations. The lake today is popular with fishermen. Rich with nutrients the lake supports trout, perch, pike and roach. Boats can be hired from the trout farm.

CONISTON

This winter scene looks peaceful enough but in past times Coniston and its fells were busy with industrial activities such as slate quarrying, copper and iron mining and charcoal production. Boats carried away the copper and iron ore. Small pleasure boats now scud around the lake. There is a ferry which criss-crosses the water, and the romantic steam launch *Gondola* makes stately tours. Today many of the former miners' cottages are used for holiday accommodation and the hills are busy with walkers.

CONISTON WATER

Early on a September morning, the peaks of The Old Man of Coniston and Wetherlam, towering above Coniston village, are reflected in the calm waters of the lake. This view from Brantwood, Ruskin's home for 28 years, was considered by him to be the finest in the Lake District. Further down the lake Arthur Ransome enjoyed a similar view while writing *Swallows and Amazons*.

WAST WATER AND THE WEST

The south-west of the Lake District contains arguably the most dramatic scenery of the region, particularly in Wasdale. Eskdale and Dunnerdale, although without lakes, are also outstanding

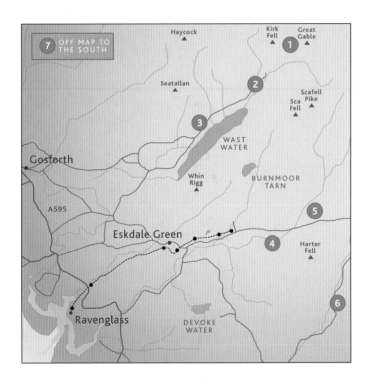

OPPOSITE – WAST WATER
The first view of Wast Water for most visitors as they approach from the west

WASDALE FROM GREAT GABLE

Westmorland Cairn, on the left, was built in 1876 by the two Westmorland brothers to mark what they felt to be the finest mountain viewpoint in the Lake District. It is hard to disagree. Lying a few hundred yards south and out of sight of the actual summit of Great Gable, it clings to the mountain's rim above a startling drop.

WASDALE

For many walkers this is the easy start of the ascent of Great Gable, on the right. The pain comes later! The summit of Kirk Fell (left) is the target for fell-runners at the annual Wasdale Show in early October. The winners manage the gruelling ascent and return in around half an hour. The tiny Church of St Olaf's, with its many mountaineering associations, is almost hidden by its protective yew trees.

WAST WATER

The mountains framing this iconic view of Wast Water are (from the left) Yewbarrow, Great Gable and Scafell Pike, the highest in England. The Screes, far right, plunge almost 2,000ft (610m) to the lake, creating a mile of unrivalled shoreline. This is England's deepest lake, but submerged on a rocky ledge there is a surprise – scores of garden gnomes, taken down by divers.

ESKDALE

The view along Upper Eskdale from the slopes of Harter Fell ends in a mountain panorama that includes the Scafell massif, Esk Pike and Bowfell. On the right is Hardknott, a fell known for the mountain pass and the strategically placed Roman fort that looks westwards down Eskdale to the sea.

HARDKNOTT FORT

Built in the 1st century AD on a grassy shelf on the side of Hardknott Fell, this Roman fort has a commanding view over mountain ranges and to the sea. It lies on the old Roman supply route linking the port at Ravenglass to Galava Fort at Ambleside. The structure is almost square with gates facing every direction. A large parade ground area and a bath block lie outside the walls.

HARTER FELL, DUDDON VALLEY

The shapely peak of Harter Fell overlooks one of the most appealing valleys of the Lake District. The valley has no lake, perhaps one reason that it remains relatively unvisited. However, the river Duddon with its rushing water, incredibly clear pools and sparkling waterfalls is more than ample compensation. Both Wordsworth and Norman Nicholson wrote poems inspired by the river.

DUDDON ESTUARY

Sandale Haws Nature Reserve, although on the edge of the shipbuilding town of Barrow-in-Furness, offers a view of mountains, pale sand and sky that could almost be Hebridean. Black Combe, lying across the estuary, is somewhat detached from the main Lake District mountains, but the views from its summit are hard to beat. The Coniston Fells are seen in the far distance on the right.

AROUND GRASMERE

Some of the prettiest and best known of the Lake District's scenery lies to the south of Dunmail Raise around Grasmere and Rydal. The characteristic profile of the Langdale Pikes is often in view

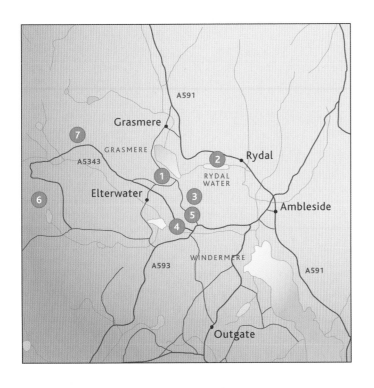

OPPOSITE – FROSTY RIVER BRATHAY
The river Brathay glides gently through beautiful meadowland after leaving Elterwater

GRASMERE

Views of Grasmere from any direction are dramatic and pretty. Seen from one of the shingle beaches on the southern shore are, from the left, Helm Crag, the pass of Dunmail Raise and the soaring slopes of Seat Sandal. Wordsworth lived in three homes around Grasmere, the most famous being Dove Cottage which is tucked away to the right of the white hotel, The Prince of Wales.

RYDAL WATER

Rydal Water lies in a sheltered bowl and early morning mists are common in fine weather. It is one of the smallest lakes and a popular walk leads around it following the western shore before crossing the river Rothay to return on a high-level path that drops into Rydal village past Rydal Mount, Wordsworth's final home.

LOUGHRIGG TARN

The soft reedy fringes of Loughrigg Tarn become ever more attractive with water lilies in the summer. The tarn hugs the side of Loughrigg Fell and the view from that side provides a perfect cameo of the Langdale Pikes. It is especially gorgeous in evening light. The National Trust owns a clutch of pretty white cottages that overlook the tarn.

ELTERWATER

There is very little access to this, the smallest of the lakes. However, a little gravel beach on the east shore, where the river Brathay starts, is a good spot to picnic and savour this view of the Langdale Pikes. The name 'Elter' derives from the Norse and means 'swan' and these birds will often glide to the shore to see if you are prepared to share your sandwiches.

RIVER BRATHAY

The gentle scenery along the river Brathay after it has left Elterwater is reflected in the river's placid pools. However a few hundred yards downstream, the pace suddenly quickens before the river thunders over Skelwith Force. This photograph, taken in mid December when there are few visitors, shows the Lake District at its most peaceful. As with the river, it is the lull before the busy period of Christmas and New Year.

BLEA TARN

Wheelchair and buggy-users are able to enjoy this magnificent view of the Langdale Pikes along the National Trust's well prepared path leading from the little car park. This is one of three 'Blea Tarns' but the only one to have a copse of conifers, adding to its upland charm. The curiously-shaped fell on the right is Side Pike.

GREAT LANGDALE

The Langdale Pikes (in the centre) rise with surprising abruptness from the level valley floor. The area abounds in colourful names – the Pikes themselves are Pike O'Stickle and Harrison Stickle (right). Further right is Pavey Ark, Lakeland's biggest cliff, which is cut through by Jack's Rake, a wonderfully challenging 'path'. Beneath is the sombrely named Dungeon Ghyll. On the skyline, to the left, are Crinkle Crags and Bow Fell.

THE ULLSWATER AREA

The long ribbon of Ullswater is the main focus of the north-eastern area. The mountainous head of the valley is dominated by Helvellyn. The main road continues past Brothers Water before twisting up Kirkstone Pass

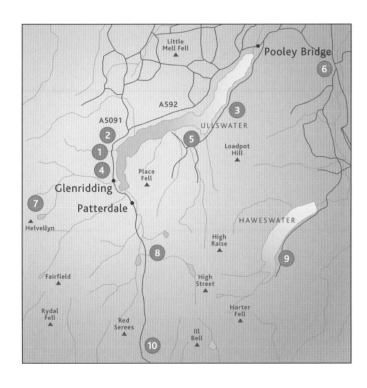

OPPOSITE – LANTY'S TARN

A short sharp climb from Glenridding leads to this lovely shallow tarn. Close by is the little knoll of Keldas. From its summit there is a wonderful view of Ullswater

GLENCOYNE FARM, ULLSWATER

The fat chimneystacks are a typical feature of old Lakeland farmhouses. There are two theories as to why the stacks were round: one that their shape was better for drawing smoke, the other that, 'Square ones are better for the devil to hide in'. This view is from the path to the former miners' cottages at Seldom Seen in Glencoynedale. It was a favourite of Queen Victoria and she may well have been amused had she known it would be so little changed, well over a century later.

WORDSWORTH'S DAFFODILS

After walking along the Glencoyne shoreline of Ullswater, Dorothy Wordsworth wrote in her diary entry of 15th April 1802, 'I never saw daffodils so beautiful...' William, her brother, included some of her description in his poem *I wandered lonely as a cloud*. Widely known as *Daffodils*, it is probably now the most famous poem in the English language. Because of it, many people associate the Lake District with the flower.

ULLSWATER BOATS

This photograph shows the very essence of a golden summer evening on Ullswater. The boats are close to the renowned Sharrow Bay Hotel but there are a multitude of peaceful moorings elsewhere on the lake. The Ullswater Yacht Club hosts regattas and the Lord Birkett Memorial Event in July is an especially wonderful sight, with over 200 boats chasing up and down the lake in full sail.

ULLSWATER SUNRISE

The golds and pinks of the sunrise over the distant Pennines are in contrast with the dark clouds massed over Ullswater. The strong silhouette of Silver Point at the base of Place Fell looms on the right. As the old saying goes, 'Red sky at night, shepherd's delight, red sky in the morning, shepherd's warning.' By mid-morning, it was raining!

THE OLD CHURCH
OF St MARTIN

MARTINDALE

The ancient yew sheltering the atmospheric Old Church of St Martin's could be older than Christendom. From the small-paned windows of its simple interior the church offers a perfectly framed view up this wild valley. The Nab is the snow-capped fell on the right. This is home to a herd of wild red deer. The Old Church is always open but only occasionally used for services.

ASKHAM

The pretty cottages in the village of Askham line an unusually long and wide village green. The road through the village climbs steadily for nearly a mile from Askham Church, by the bridge over the river Lowther, to the gateway of Askham Fell. Most of the cottages were built towards the end of the 17th century and many have impressive date stones.

STRIDING EDGE

Certainly the best known mountain ridge in the Lake District, this dramatic route to the summit of Helvellyn is climbed by many thousands each year. The narrow path with great drops on both sides can be dangerous – especially in high winds or icy conditions. On the left is Red Tarn (here emphatically not red!) so-called because it reflects the rosy glow of dawn when seen from the summit.

HARTSOP AND BROTHERS WATER

A track connects the tiny village of Hartsop to Patterdale and Ullswater. Initially the path climbs behind the village where there is this dramatic view across to Brothers Water and Hartsop Hall, sheltered by the slopes of High Hartsop Dodd. Formerly busy with milling and mining, Hartsop is now a peaceful and attractive place but hints of its industrial heritage are plentiful.

HAWESWATER

A long narrow road leads up to the head of Haweswater, but beyond this point the two rocky mountain passes of Gatesgarth and Nan Bield are definitely not for cars! The reservoir of Haweswater was constructed in the l930s by building the massive dam wall at Burnbanks and enlarging the existing lake. The reservoir supplies Manchester with drinking water. A path follows the entire length of the further shore and gives access to The Rigg (centre) and Kidsty Pike (right).

KIRKSTONE PASS

Snowdrifts take on a beautifully sculptured appearance when snow is blown into the lee of walls during blizzards. Once the road has been cleared by the snowplough, scores of people head for the top of the pass and the Kirkstone Inn becomes the hub of a mini ski resort. Families enjoy tobogganing, making snowmen and snowball fights, whilst the serious walkers strap on their crampons.

DERWENT WATER & BASSENTHWAITE

Derwent Water and Keswick, with their impressive backdrop of Skiddaw, have many literary connections. The area is lively with throngs of visitors enjoying the bustle of Keswick and the charms of Derwent Water – for many their favourite lake. The quiet east shore of Bassenthwaite is a National Nature Reserve

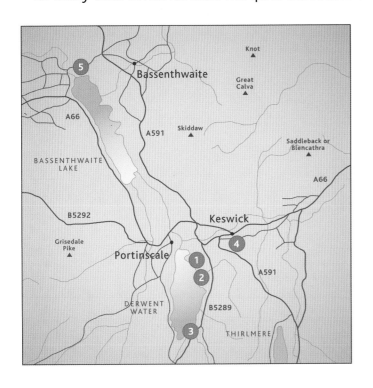

OPPOSITE – BORROWDALE
The Borrowdale valley glimpsed from the slopes of Brund Fell with the little village of Rosthwaite on the valley floor

DERWENT WATER

Mid-May can be one of the best times in the Lakes and here the cloud lifting from the fells heralds a beautiful day. Derwent Island on the left is owned by the National Trust and is the largest of the lake's islands. Occasional open days during the summer allow the public to visit the island and the restored boathouse. The hall, with its unique view up the lake, is tenanted but opens on these days.

DERWENT WATER DAWN

This view from Friar's Crag across Derwent Water to Borrowdale was a favourite of Ruskin, his first visit being in the company of his nurse at the age of five. Today numerous visitors of all ages are able to enjoy it using the simple short walk past Keswick's landing-stages. St Herbert's Island, on the right, had a Gothic hermitage whose occupant was immortalised by Wordsworth.

DERWENT WATER SUNSET

The first snows of winter coat the summit of Skiddaw, in the distance across the lake. On the right the Ashness launch landing-stage is one of seven around the lake. The traditional teak launches operate a frequent service throughout the year. The 12 mile (19km) circuit of the lake is too long for many walkers but making use of the launches offers a variety of excellent shorter walks between stages.

CASTLERIGG STONE CIRCLE

Little is known about the origins and purpose of this spectacular stone circle but its atmospheric upland setting surrounded by some of the area's highest mountains fires the imagination. Thirty-eight stones form a rough oval, within which there is an unusual small rectangular setting of another 10 stones. The photograph shows the range of mountains leading to the distant summit of Helvellyn on the right.

BASSENTHWAITE

Rich evening light illuminates the slopes of Skiddaw (left). Bassenthwaite is a National Nature Reserve and now is home to a pair of breeding ospreys. Its peaceful reedy east shore has abundant birdlife and, in summer, the east shore is particularly blessed with great drifts of wildflowers. Interesting visits can be made to the little lakeside church of St Bega and historic Mirehouse with its unusual 'bee garden'.

AROUND BUTTERMERE

The north-west area includes some of the quietest, least commercialised parts of the Lake District as well as the only coastal stretch of Cumbrian coastline with cliffs

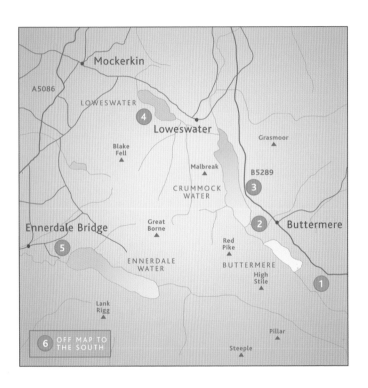

OPPOSITE – MISTY BUTTERMERE
The high fells around Buttermere are shrouded in early morning mist

BUTTERMERE

Buttermere is the topmost of three lakes beautifully strung along the same valley. The popular two-hour walk around the lake is an excellent introduction to this area. Parking is limited at this, the eastern end of the lake, but some is available here at Gatesgarth Farm. The little village of Buttermere, with its superbly situated church, two inns and a tea room, lies at the far end of the lake.

MELBREAK AND CRUMMOCK WATER

Despite the apparent calm of this photograph, two of the fells surrounding Crummock Water are particularly wild and steep. Melbreak, shown on the left with its forbidding slopes, is matched beyond by Grasmoor. The slope on the right of the photograph – colourful with the characteristic glow of dead bracken – is part of Rannerdale Knotts which, in contrast to its giant neighbours, offers a gentler climb to an attractive summit ridge.

RANNERDALE BLUEBELLS

The little valley of Rannerdale is well known for the bluebells which carpet the slopes in May and early June. In addition there are lovely hawthorn trees bearing May blossom. Rannerdale is a side valley leading from Crummock Water, very close to a rocky promontory. The lakeside road now cuts around its base. This strategic point was the site of a battle where Norman invaders were ambushed and routed by the English.

LOWESWATER

A beautiful path leads to the south-western shore of Loweswater following it for a little distance. After Watergate Farm, it leads through the mature native trees of Holme Wood then past the National Trust bothy (which can be rented for holidays). Here the small gravel beach enjoys this serene lake view. Rowing boats, especially popular with trout fishermen, can be rented from the farm.

ENNERDALE

This is the most westerly and probably the remotest of the lakes. Road access to Ennerdale is by a network of tiny lanes. The lake itself is unique in having no paved road following any shoreline. The head of the lake is somewhat dominated by Forestry Commission plantations but good access has been ensured with a variety of forest walks. Pillar, the mountain on the right, is one of the most remote Lakeland peaks.

ST BEES

Although not strictly in the Lake District, this little town, with its remarkable priory, its sandy beach and fine sandstone headland is a popular contrasting destination for Lake District visitors. On clear days the coast of Scotland and the mountains of the Isle of Man can be seen across the Irish Sea.

First published in 2006 by Myriad Books Limited, 35 Bishopsthorpe Road, London SE26 4PA

Photographs and text copyright © Val Corbett

Val Corbett has asserted her right under the Copyright, Designs and Patents Act 1998 to be identified as the author of this work.

ISBN 1 904 736 22 X   Designed by Phillip Appleton   Printed in China   www.myriadbooks.com